NOT MY WORDS

The simplest handbook to help rediscover
your direct connection to God.

S.S. Mirmont

Mirmont Publishing, Ink.

ISBN-13: 978-1-954475-49-6

Cover design by: Art Painter
Library of Congress Control Number: 2018675309
Printed in the United States of America

CONTENTS

INTRODUCTION

This is not a book.
Not really.

It is a reminder.
A mirror.
A map back to what you already know.

The words in these pages are not mine.
They are yours.
They are the whispers you've ignored, the gut feelings you've overridden, the truths you've silenced in favor of what the world told you to be.

I don't come to teach.
I come to *un-teach*.

Because what you seek—peace, purpose, meaning, God—does not live in another doctrine or another guru or another system.
It lives where it always has: inside you.

But we forget.
We all do.

We're born with connection.
Then the world begins its slow campaign to overwrite it.
We trade nature for noise.
Stillness for stimulation.
Presence for personality.
And we begin to drift.

This is not about converting you.

It's not about convincing you.
It's not even about changing you.

It's about returning you.
To Source.
To silence.
To simplicity.
To truth.

You won't need to agree with every word in this book.
You won't need to memorize anything.
You'll only need to feel what stirs when something true touches
something buried inside you.

If these words resonate, it's because they were already written on
your soul.
I'm just helping you read them again.

So take your time.
Pause where it feels heavy.
Breathe where it feels light.
Walk away and come back if needed.

There is no rush.
No score.
No perfect reader.

Only this:

You were made by something greater.
You are still connected to it.
And it is waiting for you to remember.

These are not my words.
They are yours.

— S.

PROLOGUE

Before you begin, take a breath.

This is not a book you need to finish in one sitting.
It is not something to study or analyze.
It is not something to debate.

It is a gentle return.

Each page is a door.
Each chapter is a window back to something you've forgotten—
not because you failed,
but because the world taught you to forget.

If you're tired of noise,
of pressure,
of being told who you are and how to find peace—

Then this is for you.

You don't need to believe anything.
You don't need to become anything.
You don't even need to agree.

You only need to pause…
and listen for the voice inside that says:

"Yes. I remember."

CHAPTER 1: THE SOURCE

You are not lost.
You are simply removed.

Removed from the source, the origin, the very spark that first gave rise to you.
Like a river that has forgotten it began as rain.
Like a flame that forgot it was once the sun.

The Creator gave us all things freely.
Life was not meant to be negotiated, packaged, or sold.
The roots of the earth were meant to nourish you directly—without interference.

But man has grown clever.
Too clever for truth.
And in his cleverness, he built systems.
Chains made of convenience.
Words made of ownership.
Factories made of forgetting.

Now we are fed by hands we cannot see,
From places we cannot go,
Eating things we do not recognize.

They call it progress.
But what is it, if not distance?

The Illusion of Nourishment

Protein.

The word has become sacred in modern nutrition.
People kneel at its altar. Count it. Track it. Obsess over it.

And yet, even this—our body's fuel—has been sold to us with middlemen.

We are told: eat the cow. Eat the pig. Eat the chicken.
That is where your strength comes from.

But who told you that?
Did God say, "You must consume the flesh of another to be whole?"
Or did He offer you every green thing that grows from the earth?

Even the beasts you are told to eat—where do they find their strength?

The cow eats grass.
The elephant eats roots and leaves.
The gorilla—your genetic cousin—feasts on fruit and flowers.

They are strong because they go to the source.
Not because they consume each other.

You have been tricked.
Taught to consume the consumer.
Fed a lie that keeps you tethered to death, and not to life.

The cow is not the source.
The pig is not the source.
The chicken is not the source.

They are middlemen.

And middlemen, in spiritual terms, are interference.

Kingdom Law

In the wild, nothing is wasted.
Every creature plays a part in the cycle.
There is death, yes. But it is sacred. Rare. Honored.

Humans, however, turned this rhythm into routine.
We industrialized the sacrifice.
We outsourced the killing.
We removed ourselves from the consequences of our desire.

This is not evil by accident.
It is evil by design.

It is a slow removal from Source.
From the direct channel between your body and your God.

You do not need the middleman.
You never did.

Return to What Grows

You were designed to be sustained by the living.
Not the dead.

You were offered herbs, seeds, grains, roots, and fruits.
All still pulsing with light, even after they are picked.
They are not robbed of life—they *offer* it.

Science calls it chlorophyll.
Mystics call it divine energy.
God called it good.

Eat that which gives.
Not that which had to be taken.

Eat that which lives in the sun.
Not that which dies in the dark.

Eat that which your Creator placed in your reach—without blood, without guilt, without death.

This is the first doorway back to the Source.

A Simple Practice

Today, walk into a grocery store, a farmer's market, or your own backyard.

Pause.

Look at every item and ask:

Did this come from the Source?
Or from the middleman?

Then choose.
Not with guilt.
With gratitude.
With remembrance.

Let your body be a temple.
And let only that which was offered freely enter it.

CHAPTER 2: THE MIDDLE MAN

A child does not need a translator to feel love.
A deer does not need a priest to find water.
A tree does not need a screen to know the sun.

And yet—
Here we are, surrounded by middlemen.
Gatekeepers of every kind.
Between you and your food.
Between you and your breath.
Between you and your God.

This is not how it was meant to be.

Suffering Is Separation

Let it be known:

All who are separated from the Source shall suffer.
Not by punishment.
But by distance.

If you block the sun from a plant, it will wither.
If you dam the river, it will rot.
If you obstruct the truth, your soul will ache.

Modern suffering is not just emotional.
It is spiritual dislocation.
A life pulled off course by countless hands claiming to help.

They tell you who you are.

They sell you what you need.
They offer you salvation—but always with terms.

This is the true pain of modern life:

We are starving at the table, because we have mistaken the waiter for the cook.

The Industrial Lie

Look at what has become of food.

Where once you picked berries with your own hands, now you pick plastic off the shelf.
Where once you grew herbs under the sun, now you trust factories with fluorescent lights.

The cow is born in a cage.
Fed what it was never meant to eat.
Pumped full of fear, then slaughtered in silence.

And you eat it—not knowing its name, its pain, its purpose.
You bless the meal, but you do not know what you're blessing.

You are not just consuming flesh.
You are consuming disconnection.

You are eating the system.
And the system is the middleman.

Beyond Food

It is not just in your meals.
It is in your meaning.

You seek peace—so you scroll.
You seek joy—so you buy.
You seek truth—so you search engines, not your soul.

But truth cannot be bought, bottled, branded, or borrowed.
It can only be *remembered.*

You cannot pay a pastor to know God for you.
You cannot follow a guru into your own soul.
You cannot rent salvation.

Middlemen promise shortcuts.
But every shortcut takes you further from yourself.

What Must Be Removed

To return to truth, you must begin to remove the middleman.
Gently. Intentionally. Constantly.

This is not an act of rebellion.
It is an act of remembering.

- When you feel pain, don't numb it with pills—sit with it.

- When you feel hunger, ask what your soul is starving for.

- When you feel confused, don't Google it—breathe, and ask the Source directly.

Even in silence, answers come.
Especially in silence.

You Are Not Alone

The world is loud, but truth is still speaking.
Not through ads, not through headlines, not through public figures.

But through still water.
Through wind in trees.
Through the ache in your own chest when something doesn't feel right.

That is the voice of God.
That is the Source.

It has been drowned out by a thousand middlemen.
But it has not disappeared.

You do not need to run.
You need only to remove.

Strip away what you were told.
Peel back what you were sold.
And sit—barefoot, unbranded, and listening.

The Source will speak.

CHAPTER 3: ROOTS

Remembering is the hardest part.
Forgetting? That's easy.
Forgetting is the default.
It begins the moment we are born.

The world is loud with lies.
Soft truths are drowned before they ever find voice.
By the time you can walk, you are already walking away from yourself.

This is not your fault.
But it is now your responsibility.

The Deletion Begins Early

From the first branded toy in your crib,
From the first word someone taught you to say,
From the first commercial between cartoons—

The world began to write its script on your soul.

You were not asked.
You were not warned.
But you were programmed.

You were told what is valuable.
What is beautiful.
What is worth striving for.

And so you began to forget:

- The taste of wild berries.

- The feel of dirt between your fingers.

- The sound of your own thoughts.

- The voice of your Creator, which once lived inside you like breath.

Imagine This

Close your eyes.

Now picture this:

You are born in nature.
There are no words.
No schedules.
No walls.
No screens.
No one tells you what is important.

Your parents do not speak, but they love.
They protect.
They feed you from the land.
You sleep under stars.
You wake with the sun.
You drink from spring water.
You eat with your hands.
You cry when you need.
You laugh without reason.

There is no name for you, yet you are known.
There is no mirror, yet you are whole.
There is no clock, yet time bends to your joy.

This is not fantasy.
This is memory.
You are not imagining paradise.
You are remembering your roots.

Enlightenment = To Lighten

We are not here to become more.

We are here to become *less*—
Less burdened.
Less distracted.
Less heavy.

Enlightenment isn't about learning something new.
It is about lightening what you carry.
Letting go of all that is not truth.

To lighten the mind.
To lighten the body.
To lighten the soul.

To walk as the trees do—
Rooted, but rising.
Still, but alive.

Truth Is Constant

There is a way to recognize truth.

Truth is not trendy.
It does not shift with opinion polls or social movements.
It does not require updates.

That which is constant is truth.
That which changes with mood, market, or moment—is not.

Light is constant.
It exists whether you see it or not.
Whether the room is lit or dark, light is still possible.

The sun does not cease to burn just because clouds cover your sky.

So it is with truth.

The truth is not missing.
You are.

Constant vs. Constructed

Let us name it plainly:

- A tree that grows in nature = Constant truth
- A plastic tree in a shopping mall = Constructed illusion
- Dirt beneath your feet = Constant truth
- Pavement = Constructed illusion
- Living fruit from a branch = Constant truth
- Flesh from a slaughtered animal = Constructed interference

You were born knowing the difference.
You were taught to ignore it.

Now you must *unlearn* the illusion.
Peel it back like a label on a product that never served you.

The Tree That Gives

The tree bears fruit and lives on.
It is not harmed by giving.
It does not suffer when picked.
It does not mourn what it offers.

This is how the Creator works.

Always giving.
Never ending.
Always enough.

You may eat from the tree for decades,
And still it blooms.
Even in winter, it rests with dignity,
So it may return in spring with more to offer.

The fruit that gives without loss
is the mirror of divine love.

The Flesh That Dies

The animal gives—but only once.
Its life must end for your meal to begin.

This is not how the Creator designed daily sustenance.

Death is not evil.
It is sacred.
It is part of the great cycle.

But to industrialize death...
To consume it without reverence...
To treat life as meat-on-demand...
This is interference.

And this interference
is where suffering begins.

A Law Unspoken

If you have access to the living gifts of the earth—
herbs, roots, seeds, rice, fruit, and grain—

Then you are called to eat from the Source.
Not from death.
Not from the middleman.

This is not a restriction.
It is a restoration.

A return to the Garden you never truly left.
Only forgot.

You are not being asked to change who you are.
You are being asked to remember who you've always been.

CHAPTER 4: TRUTH IS CONSTANT

Truth does not change.

It is not a mood.
It is not a wave.
It is not a feeling, nor a trend, nor a belief.

Truth is not "true for you" and something else "true for me."
That is preference.
That is perspective.
That is experience—not truth.

Truth is what remains when everything else is stripped away.

It was true before you arrived.
It will be true after you leave.
It does not need your agreement to exist.

How to Know the Real

We are surrounded by shifting sands.

Headlines.
Opinion pieces.
Social feeds.
Religious interpretations.
Scientific studies that contradict last year's studies.

And yet, deep inside you, something still *knows.*

Something still remembers what is *real.*

Constant = Truth
Inconsistent = Illusion

This is the key.

Examples the Soul Recognizes

- **Light**
  The light exists whether or not your eyes are open.
  Whether the lamp is on or off.
  The power was always there.
  Your involvement is optional.

- **Nature**
  The tree grows regardless of your attention.
  The ocean crashes without your permission.
  A seed becomes a sprout without a single word spoken.

- **Love**
  Not romance. Not possession. Not transaction.
  But the quiet, patient love that gives with no expectation.
  It does not vanish with time.
  It is constant.

These are signs.
These are fingerprints of the Divine.
They do not need verification.
They simply *are.*

False Truths: The Beautiful Imitations

Now consider the imitations:

- **Electric light**
  It requires wires, switches, power grids, and your hand.
  Without these, the room remains dark.
  It resembles the sun, but it is not the sun.

- **Synthetic trees**
  Beautiful, perhaps. Durable, perhaps.

But without roots. Without life.
They are sculptures, not beings.

- **Factory food**
  It resembles nourishment.
  It fills your belly but empties your body of vitality.
  It is taste engineered to mimic the real.

These are unstable truths.
They imitate life but require your constant maintenance to survive.

Truth does not require your support to remain alive.
Illusion does.

The Creator's Signature

God's work is not loud.
It does not shout.
It does not market itself.
It simply exists.

Like gravity.
Like breath.
Like light.

You don't have to understand gravity to stand upright.
You don't have to worship air to breathe.

So it is with the Creator.

He made systems that do not need your permission to work.
He made truth that cannot be edited or upgraded.

When Man Tries to Play God

Man can mimic.
He can create plastic trees, artificial light, processed love.
He can market the illusion so well you begin to believe it's better than the real thing.

But man can only copy.
He cannot create the source.
He cannot grow an apple from nothing.
He cannot command light from the sun.

He can build temples, but not heaven.
He can make machines, but not souls.

Every illusion requires a salesman.
Truth requires only silence.

The Compass Within

You already have a compass for truth.

It lives in your gut.
It pulses behind your ribs.
It tightens when something is wrong.
It softens when something is real.

That is God's voice, without words.
That is the constant signal of the Source.

The world may call it instinct.
But we know it's remembering.

So Ask Yourself

Every time you make a decision, choose a path, absorb a teaching, or speak:

Is this **constant**, or is it **reactive**?
Did this **exist before me**, or is it built around my preferences?
Does this **set me free**, or does it ask me to obey?

If the answer aligns with life, light, love, and simplicity—
It is likely Truth.

If the answer depends on your mood, identity, validation, or conformity—
It is likely not.

You are not being asked to believe harder.
You are being asked to remember more softly.

Truth is not missing.
It is simply waiting to be seen again.

CHAPTER 5: THE TREE AND THE FLESH

A tree does not cry out when you pluck its fruit.
It does not recoil.
It does not die.

It gives—season after season, year after year—without demand, without condition.
It asks for nothing but sunlight and soil.
And still, it offers sweetness.

This is Divine.

This is how your Creator designed life to give itself to life.

Now compare this to the animal.
The flesh.
The one who must be taken.
The one who does not survive the offering.

This is the difference between **the tree** and **the flesh**.
Between what *gives* and what must be *taken*.

Life Meant to Give

The tree is a teacher.

It bears its fruit without ego.
It rests in winter, and gives again in spring.
It blesses the world through presence alone.

The apple does not scream when picked.

The fig does not flee.
The orange does not hide.

Even when the fruit falls to the ground untouched,
the tree still gives.
It does not hoard.
It does not regret.

This is how you were meant to live.
This is how you were meant to be fed.

"From every tree of the garden you may freely eat…"
(*Genesis 2:16*)

It was the first nourishment given to mankind.
It is still enough.

Life That Must Be Taken

The animal is sacred too.
Created by the same hands.
Warmed by the same breath.
Animated by the same spark.

But to consume its body is to end its presence.

The lamb does not volunteer its neck.
The cow does not give you its flesh joyfully.
The fish does not leap into your pan.

To eat the flesh of a creature
is to take what it cannot give.

And yes, it may sustain you.
In times of need, in wilderness, in emergency—
even ancient laws made space for such consumption.

But it was never meant to be your daily ritual.
Not by divine design.
Only by human invention.

The Interference of Industry

What once was sacred is now sanitized.
What once was rare is now routine.

Wrapped in cellophane.
Chilled and packaged.
Slaughtered while you sleep.
Marketed while you scroll.

You are not asked to feel.
You are only asked to buy.

This is not connection.
This is not reverence.
This is forgetting.

The middleman has not only inserted himself—he has covered your eyes.

You don't see the creature.
You don't hear the final breath.
You don't touch the blood.
You don't bless the life taken.

You simply consume.
And move on.

But your soul remembers.
It always does.

A Divine Distinction

To eat from the tree is to join the cycle.
To take from the flesh is to disrupt it.

One nourishes without loss.
The other nourishes only through death.

One reflects the giving nature of God.
The other reflects the appetite of man.

This is not condemnation.
This is invitation.

To return.
To remember.
To see clearly again.

When Is Flesh Permissible?

There is an unwritten law.
You know it deep within you.

It says:

"Thou shall not eat meat unless—
you have no access to herbs, seeds, grains, rice, or root veg."

This is not scripture.
This is conscience.
This is the law written not on tablets,
but in the chambers of the heart.

You are not called to perfection.
You are called to awareness.

If you are stranded, eat what you must.
If you are blessed with choice, choose what gives freely.

What You Eat Is What You Align With

The tree gives and lives.
So does the vine.
So does the plant.
So does the spring.

Eat these, and you align with life.

The flesh must die.
The blood must be spilled.
The breath must end.

Eat these regularly, and something in you becomes numb to the cost.

Remember This

You were not born hungry for blood.
You were taught to crave it.
You were told it made you strong.

But the strongest beings in the kingdom—the elephant, the ox, the gorilla—eat plants.

They go to the source.

So must you.

Not as punishment.
But as return.

CHAPTER 6: THE BABY ALWAYS KNOWS

The baby is the most honest soul you'll ever meet.
Not because it speaks well—
But because it speaks *without words.*

The baby sees.
The baby feels.
The baby *knows.*

It does not weigh your résumé.
It does not care for your title.
It cannot be fooled by charm, power, or wealth.

Because the baby is still fresh from the Source.

It has not yet been taught how to lie to itself.

The Purity of Undistorted Judgment

The baby has no religion.
No ideology.
No "correct" worldview.

It has only truth.

And it recognizes truth without needing a definition.

- When you are anxious, the baby feels it.

- When you are angry, the baby shrinks.

- When you lie, the baby cries.

- When you love, the baby glows.

It is not guessing.
It is not reacting.

It is *responding to resonance.*

Your vibration is not hidden.
Not from a baby.
Not from God.
And not from yourself, if you stop to listen.

The Baby as Mirror

You can tell who someone *truly is* by how babies respond to them.

Watch carefully:

- A baby will often cry when surrounded by unstable energy.

- A baby will laugh freely in the presence of a soul at peace.

- A baby will reach toward the one who feels safe—without ever hearing a word.

That is the measurement of truth.
Not debate. Not proof. Not prestige.
But response.

A Story of Two Faces

Imagine this:

A man walks into the room. He smiles at you. He shakes your hand. He speaks kindly.
But then he turns to your assistant, or your waiter, or your child—and is cold, dismissive, cruel.

What kind of man is this?

A man of *unstable truth.*
A man who shifts like mood and convenience.

A man who has trained himself to perform, not to *be*.

The baby sees both faces.
And will not clap for either.

Why the Baby Knows

Because the baby has not yet been taught to ignore what it feels.

It does not have filters.
It does not have dogma.
It does not have trauma-coded programming yet.

It is not looking for status.
It is not impressed by language.

It is scanning for energy.
And it *knows* the difference between peace and performance.

Be Seen Like a Baby Sees

If you want to know how close you are to the Source,
watch how children respond to you.

Not because they are perfect—
But because they are still *clear.*

Their vision is not blurred by years of justification, defense, ambition, pain, and ego.

They feel before they think.

And God speaks through that feeling.

The Baby is the Reminder

We are not told to become scholars, sages, or saints.

We are told to become *like little children.*

Why?

Because children trust the light.

They resist the fake.
They cry at injustice.
They laugh at simplicity.
They know when someone is unstable—even when adults cannot see it.

The baby always knows.

A Simple Practice

The next time you hold a child, sit with one, or even see one from afar:

- **Pause.**

- **Notice your energy.**

- **Don't perform.**

- **Just be.**

Let the child show you who you are in that moment.

Not through their words,
but through their eyes.

You may find yourself revealed.

You may also find yourself returning.

CHAPTER 7: MOOD

Mood is the most overlooked barrier between you and the Source.

It is internal, invisible, and slippery.
It disguises itself as truth.
It convinces you: *"This is just how I feel, so it must be real."*

But mood is not truth.
Mood is weather.
It passes.

And if you build your life in the storm,
don't be surprised when it washes away everything sacred.

Truth Is Constant. Mood Is Not.

The Creator is constant.
The earth spins whether you're joyful or bitter.
The sun rises whether you're laughing or grieving.

"I am the LORD, I change not."
(Malachi 3:6)

If God is stable…
If Truth is stable…
Then the further you swing from stability,
the further you are from the Source.

Mood is the movement.
Truth is the anchor.

What Happens When You Break From Stability

- You raise your voice.

- You justify your temper.

- You speak words you don't mean.

- You believe things that aren't real.

- You act out of fear, ego, or defense.

And then?
You call it "authentic."
You call it "passion."
You call it "human."

Yes, it is human.
But it is not *divine.*

The more attached you are to your moods,
the more easily you are manipulated—by media, by people, by pain.

Mood is the devil's steering wheel.

The Argument Trap

Arguments are not born in truth.
They are born in mood.

One person shifts.
The other reacts.
Soon, both are defending versions of themselves that don't even exist anymore.

The quieter one usually sees it:
"This isn't about what we said.
This is about how we felt when we said it."

Truth does not argue.
Truth simply stands.

When you are in a mood, you cannot see clearly.
When you cannot see clearly, you cannot speak truth.
When you cannot speak truth, you disconnect from the Source.

This is the trap.

Mood Is Not the Problem—Attachment To It Is

You will feel.
You are made to feel.
God did not make you numb.

But you were never meant to become your feelings.
You were never meant to *stay* in them.
You were never meant to follow every emotion like a compass.

Feelings are not North Stars.
They are signals—nothing more.

The longer you stay in a mood,
the more distorted your truth becomes.

Stability Is Sacred

A man who is stable cannot be bought.
He cannot be baited.
He cannot be moved by flattery or threats.

This man is a mirror of the Creator.

He does not swing with opinion.
He does not fight for approval.
He listens before he reacts.
He sees clearly, and he speaks rarely.

This man's presence heals rooms.
Because his energy is not for sale.

Be like this.

Not passive.
Not robotic.
But *anchored.*

A Simple Practice

When you feel your mood shift:

1. **Stop.**
    Say nothing. Do nothing. Don't decide. Don't defend.

2. **Breathe.**
    Inhale deeply through the nose.
    Hold.
    Exhale slowly through the mouth.
    Repeat. Let the weather pass.

3. **Ask:**
    Is this me?
    Or is this just a passing cloud?

4. **Wait for the calm.**
    Then speak.
    Then choose.
    Then act.

Why This Matters

Truth requires stillness.
Stillness requires stability.
Stability begins where mood ends.

If you are constantly shifting,
how will the still small voice of God ever find you?

Be still.
Return.
Anchor yourself.

Not because you're perfect.
But because the Source is.

CHAPTER 8: ASSOCIATIONS

You are not your name.
You are not your job.
You are not your history, your trauma, or your triumphs.
You are not your religion.
You are not your beliefs.
You are not your face, your title, your passport, or your bloodline.

You are not even your body.

These are all **attachments.**
And attachment is the great illusion.

The Labels You've Been Given

From birth, you were assigned identities like clothes:

- Boy. Girl.

- Smart. Slow.

- Shy. Wild.

- American. Iranian. Christian. Muslim. Spiritual-but-not-religious.

Each one wrapped around your soul like a thread.
Each one added a layer between you and God.

Some labels seemed useful. Some felt beautiful.
But even the beautiful ones—especially the beautiful ones—are prisons if they keep you from returning to the source of who you

truly are.

The more words you need to describe yourself,
the further you've wandered from the truth.

The Name Trap

Even your name is not truly yours.

It was given before you understood meaning.
It was spoken before you had a choice.

Your name is useful in this world.
But it is not who you are.

When Moses asked God, "Who shall I say sent me?"
God did not say, "Tell them I'm Yahweh, Son of X, affiliated with Y,
voted Z."

God said simply:

"I Am."

That's it.

The most powerful identity is *no identity at all.*

Identity Is Not Connection

To identify is to separate.
To associate is to isolate.

When you say:

- "I am a Republican."

- "I am vegan."

- "I am a mother."

- "I am a Christian."

- "I am Iranian-American."

- "I am a victim."
- "I am successful."

You create a wall between you and those who are not.

You create division where there was once only light.

You don't need a label to belong to the Divine.
You were never asked to present credentials.

You only need to be.

Detach to Return

This is not about erasing your experience.
It's about unbinding your essence.

Try this:

Imagine erasing your job title.
Then your nationality.
Then your political stance.
Then your gender.
Then your religion.
Then your name.

What's left?

Only this:
I am.

And that is enough.

Because the moment you return to **I am**,
you return to God.

But What About Family?

Even your relationship to others must be released to reach the deepest truth.

Your mother is your mother by biology, yes.

But she is also a soul—on her own journey.
So are your children.
So is your partner.

They do not own you.
You do not own them.

You belong to God.
They belong to God.
That is enough.

Why Association is Slavery

Every time you associate yourself with something made by man—
you inherit that thing's flaws.

Associate with a religion,
and you carry its dogma.

Associate with a country,
and you carry its sins.

Associate with your trauma,
and you inherit its limitations.

These become the new middlemen.
They convince you that to know God,
you must first come through *them.*

But there are no intermediaries.
No passwords.
No entry fee.

Only the silence of: **I am.**

A Simple Practice

Today, try this:

1.   **Write your name.**
      Say it aloud. Look at it on paper.

2. **Then cross it out.**
   Gently. As if thanking it for its service, but letting it go.

3. **Say aloud:**
   "I am not this name. I am not this story. I am."

4. **Sit in that space.**
   Not as a person.
   Not as a role.
   Not as a title.
   But as being itself.

You are not disappearing.
You are returning.

When you strip away what is not you,
you will finally remember what always was.

I am.
That is enough.
That is the source.
That is God.

CHAPTER 9:
OUTDOOR LIVING

Nature does not argue.
It does not beg for attention.
It simply *is.*

It is the original scripture.
The only temple built without hands.
The only place untouched by ego.

God's fingerprint is in every branch,
every blade of grass,
every cloud that floats across your ceiling of sky.

If you want to find your way back to the Source,
step outside.

You Were Made for This

Your skin was designed for sunlight.
Your lungs for clean air.
Your feet for soil.

You were never meant to be indoors all day.
Never meant to sit under flickering lights.
Never meant to breathe recycled air and forget the scent of rain.

Your body is a compass.
It aches when removed from the earth.
It softens when returned.

You may have forgotten—but your cells remember.

Concrete Is Not Sacred

You cannot hear God through a television.
You cannot smell truth on a freeway.

Your environment matters.

You can eat the right food, think the right thoughts, read the right books—
but if you are disconnected from the rhythm of nature,
your spirit will still be hungry.

A tree does not thrive indoors.
Neither do you.

The Devil's Playground

The modern world is a carefully constructed trap.
Its comfort is not rest—it is distraction.
Its speed is not freedom—it is pressure.
Its noise is not music—it is distortion.

Everything that numbs you,
everything that screens you from the sky,
everything that removes you from nature—
pulls you further from the Source.

We are not saying cities are evil.
We are saying they are *interference*.

You don't need to escape the world.
You need to step into the one that was made for you.

Nature Is Not Optional

This is not lifestyle advice.
This is spiritual instruction.

If you do not walk among trees,
you will forget what it means to grow slowly.

If you do not touch the dirt,
you will forget what you were made from.

If you do not watch the stars,
you will forget how to navigate without a screen.

If you do not listen to wind,
you will forget the sound of the breath of God.

This is not poetry.
This is prescription.

A True Sign

Once, in conversation, I spoke of needing to return to living outdoors.
Moments later, a literal billboard passed before me—
its bold words reading:

"OUTDOOR LIVING"

A sign.
Not metaphor.
Literal.
Undeniable.

God is always speaking.
But some messages need sunlight to be seen.

The Body and the Earth

Your body is not just yours.
It is of the earth.
It is dust and water and fire and wind.

To treat it as separate is to dishonor both.

- When you walk barefoot on the ground,
  you close the circuit.

- When you sleep under stars,

your dreams remember ancient truths.

- When you eat from the land,
your body vibrates with memory.

Outdoor living is not a trend.
It is a return.
To sanity.
To peace.
To Source.

A Simple Practice

Today, go outside.
Even if just for 10 minutes.

- Take off your shoes.

- Sit on the grass.

- Place your hands on the earth.

- Close your eyes.

- Say nothing.

Let the soil speak.
Let the breeze remind you.
Let the sun do what no screen ever can.

You are not separate.
You are not artificial.
You are not made for fluorescent light and glass towers.

You are the wilderness.
You are part of the forest, the ocean, the field.
You are a creature of God's making.

And every time you forget,
the trees are waiting.

CHAPTER 10: REMEMBERING

If you've made it here, you've already begun.

Not because you finished a book—
But because something in you *woke up again.*

This was never about learning.
It was always about remembering.

You are not here to become something.
You are here to return to what you already are.

You Were Never Lost

Only distracted.
Only layered over.
Only filled with names, jobs, beliefs, moods, meals, systems, fears.

You are like a flame buried beneath a hundred wet blankets.
The flame never went out.
It just waited.

And now—
You are uncovering it.

This Is Not Religion

This is not a new faith.
This is not a rebellion.
This is not a self-help trick.

This is a remembering.

- Of who you were before they told you what to be.

- Of what you knew before the noise.

- Of the stillness you had before language.

- Of the voice you heard before you knew it had a name.

This is not my truth.
These are not my words.

These are yours.
They've been buried, not broken.

DO THIS NOW

You don't need a perfect moment.
You don't need the right clothes, the right book, the right incense.
You don't need anything.

You only need to act.

1. Find a quiet place in nature.
It can be a backyard, a park, a mountaintop, or even a patch of earth near the sidewalk.

2. Remove your shoes.
Let your skin meet the soil.
Let your body return to its birthplace.

3. Breathe this prayer, aloud or within:

"I release all that is not mine.
I unlearn.
I remember.
I return to You."

4. Then listen.
Not with your ears.
With your whole being.

Let the wind say what the world never could.
Let the silence say what your soul already knows.

You Will Forget Again

The world will pull you back.
Screens. Schedules. Triggers. Names. Opinions.

You'll forget again.

But that's okay.

Because the path is always here.
The door never locks.
God is not impatient.
The Source does not punish the lost.
It simply waits—unmoving, unchanging, eternal.

Every moment is an invitation to return.
Not once.
But again.
And again.
And again.

One Final Word

You are not broken.
You are not too far gone.
You do not need to be better.
You only need to be real.

Strip off what you're not.
Stand still.
And say simply:

"I am."

Then listen.

That voice you hear in the quiet?

It is not mine.
It is not yours.

It is the remembering of the Creator within you.

And it never left.

You were never disconnected. Only distracted.

Not My Words is the simplest, clearest book you'll ever read about how to find your way back to the Creator.

No dogma. No spiritual performance. No middlemen.

Just a quiet, poetic journey back to the Source—from under the noise, beyond the systems, past the labels and expectations the world handed you.

Through ten short chapters, you'll be guided to:

- Unlearn what keeps you distant from God

- Reconnect with nature, truth, and simplicity

- Let go of identity, mood, and interference

- Remember who you were before the world named you

This isn't a book of beliefs.
It's a mirror to help you see again.
The voice inside you. The voice that never left.
The one that's been waiting to speak:

"I am."

ACKNOWLEDGEMENT

I give thanks to the Creator, whose presence is constant even when I am not.
To the Source of all things—thank you for the breath, the truth, and the remembering.

To those who listened to my silence, and saw me anyway—thank you.

And to the voice within me that never stopped whispering: *"Write."*

Layout and editing by Timothy Green
Cover design by Timothy Green

ISBN: 978-1-961694-01-9

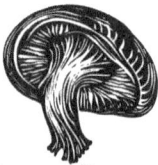

FUNGIBLE EDITIONS

First print edition by Fungible Editions
fungibleeditions.com

Also published as an NFT collectable chapbook
by Alexandria Books, 2024
alexandriabooks.com

Contents

Authors' Note

Ever since I learned about haibun, I've been transfixed. The journalistic prose, juxtaposed with haiku and a carefully chosen title, creates a vertical leap that can't be accessed in other forms. With a haibun's prismatic myriad of cuts, the hope is that this chapbook, a crown of them, feels like watching a chandelier reflect along the wall on a sunny day.

Speaking of which, let's rewind to a few days before the start of April 2024 (which is National Poetry Month). I wanted to tackle a new poetry project, but was unsure of what to do. The year before, I'd written a collectible chapbook, *Watering Can*, and I wanted a project of similar magnitude. I was bemoaning my indecision aloud as Tim and I put away the laundry together. While he matched our striped socks, he had the idea of borrowing aspects of another form that fascinates me—sonnet crowns—and the concept of a haibun crown was born. In this series, each word from the haiku is contained within the body of the next haibun, creating an interlocking chain of poems. The final jewel, the last haibun, circles back to the first by building a haiku from words in the first haibun's body. This haibun crown was written over the course of the month, with each of us writing on alternating days.

If you want to make life more exciting, I recommend being with someone that not only does the laundry with you, but also has brilliant ideas in the process. Collaborating with Tim on this project has been a therapeutic joy—with our four kids in two states, we can't spend every moment together, as we'd like, and this chapbook helps explore that. And the joy? Well, it's a constant cycle.

Pink is not only my favorite color, but also the name of April's full moon. And as for the "hot" part of the title … well some taps you have to turn on for yourself!

Here's hoping that the laundry puts itself away and that you enjoy this as much as we loved writing it,

Katie & Tim

HOT PINK MOON

A CROWN OF HAIBUN

All-in-One

The new washer/dryer came today. I vacuumed up the old
lint that never sparked a fire. Now this one machine can do
everything—the turning and the whirling in the water which
then flips to dry while the clothes all stay snuggled up inside.
I picture a pair of socks skipping through a car wash,
pinned together—a wooly kite. I ask you how this
shiny thing works, you tell me of condensers; how
the heat has a way of forging its escape.

> the ignored smoke alarm …
> finally stopped
> beeping

Phase Shift

We ignored the alarm clock preemptively, having forgotten to set it the night before. The morning was full, instead, of smoke from a dream, the forests ablaze and all of us fleeing. Between the trees, a chorus of backhoes and bulldozers beeping as they cut firebreaks through fallen timber. All of it stopped when we finally reached a clearing. The air was clean, the sunset something to behold.

> the cool side
> of the pillow
> waxing moon

Your Mom

I'm so glad *cool* made it past the '90s—but then again, tonight, under this same moon, someone plopped their head down on a pillow and said *groovy* without a thread of irony. Non-Americans always tease me when I say *Awesome*, which I totally do, while waxing the side of my Tesla—wondering if my penchant for pretending to be *The Karate Kid* is now problematic. Sometimes I worry I'm so full of slang and old jokes and vintage movies that I'm a meme with legs.

a grasshopper
leaps to the next blade—
turn of the century

Sanctuary

Every autumn, the grasshoppers would move into the garage. They'd gather near the water heater, and at the turn of a light leap to the boxes of books I'd stacked next to it. But what they loved most was the lawnmower, the ghost of the grass still haunting the gap between its deck and the cutting blade. By winter, they'd move through the cracks in the century-old foundation and climb into the walls for warmth. Their legs were a chorus of clicks in the sheetrock until that space, too, was taken by the cold. The mounds of their ancestors must have added to the insulation.

shedding with age
the exoskeleton
dance party

Seventeen Years

I'm sorry! I know there are too many poems about cicadas—
their double Cs have a way of clicking their exoskeletons right
into a poet's pen. And this year, we're bound to have so many
of them, shedding from every tree in unison; chandeliers with
phosphorescent flames. In this day and age, it's no wonder we
relate to these red-eyed outcasts; these not-quite butterflies;
these well-winged warblers—these wings as transparent
as hope at a high school dance party; where we wish
to be seen doing the electric slide in perfect unison—
and strain to remember if the door is a push or a pull
when all that's left to do is flee from inside.

time [the flow state] travel

The Great Circle

Time flows strangely as you travel between states. What are the hours to a block of ice? Yet in minutes that water's vapor will fill a room. Even the flights back and forth are confusing. Heading west wastes an hour in the air but gains two in the world's turning. As if less than nothing had been missed. Was that a dream or a daydream that you lost in the drone of the engines? Did you nod off or nod once? There are no straight lines. The shortest distance between points is an arc.

       homing
       in wherever
       we are

Stomaching It

Please do not ride the goats, says the attendant to the father
of the toothless baby grabbing bareback fistfuls of fur. I wonder
how many times she's said exactly that; how at first it was followed
by a laugh, and now she feels mostly like a megaphone or a missile,
homing her way through scat. And in the midst of all the *baas*, look
at that—a baby takes her first step just to grab a horn. And wherever
we are, the same little wobbles and the desperate need to paw.

        an empty tin can
        bobs in the pond—
        I miss you

Alchemy

The museum of natural history displays a periodic table of artifacts from the human world: crushed cans of tin, plumb bobs full of lead, the noble gasses shouting their names from an array of discharge tubes. Some of the heaviest elements no longer exist but were there once, the plaque assures us, though they decay in fractions of a second, evaporating in the empty ponds of their pedestals. *Blink and you'll miss it*, a parent says behind us, meaning childhood, I think, but she could have meant anything.

      solar eclipse
      over the clouds
      for a spell

In the Round

Somehow we live our lives between eclipses—
which is to say we've learned to play within

ellipses; how the real story unfurls backstage;
the ingénue so in love with the usher, to continue

another popcorn of a tale. Outside, a classic car
horn blares us back, to where, in pairs, lovers

used to hold hands along the track—how grapes
grab a vine. And there it is again, that curve

before it all began—just as a carousel turns, the
world yearns to see the moon top-hat the sun.

How black and white is best broken up with red
lips; and this is in the space before a spell's kiss—

which, solar-powered, travels above the clouds. But
it too must topple down: a raindrop for your mouth.

     shattering
     the fourth wall—
     a show of stars

What Did You Think We Were Talking About?

To call anything "earth-shattering" seemed like hyperbole until the fourth round that night, this time right up against the bedroom wall, so loud it must have woken all the neighbors. When it was over, they were left panting, and it felt as if the ground itself was, too, all of it shaken into heaps of debris they tread through, weak-kneed, to the window, before throwing back the curtains like the stars of a show.

its echo arrives before the word thunder

A Mile High

First, the vertigo arrives—the sense that I'm flying around the top of the mountain in a prop plane; the blade and its endless whirling. And then it's my stomach that starts hurting. My mind plunges from the plane to the muck buried in a lake. Words echo—the thunder of their meaningless wake. How did I feel before the ascent? A headache lands before I escape its descent.

    waiting
    by the window …
    the scent of pines

Another Ars Poetica

My friend the field guide is teaching me about local
pines. We're by a window overlooking the forest, waiting for a meeting to begin. A Coulter's cones are the
biggest in Norh America, she tells me. Ten pound
widow-makers. Don't park there in the fall. The
smoothest are Jeffrey's. They feel good in your hands.
Kids use them as footballs. If it's painful, it's ponderosa,
covered in barbs—but if you find one, go to the tree that
dropped it and put your nose in the bark. Sweetest scent
of vanilla. There must be a poem in that somewhere, she
says.

> forest of songbirds
> all the songs
> not songs

Crash

In the middle of the forest, the songbirds stopped singing—
first the notes from the old song hung in the air on the branches
of vibrato. Sometimes the start of rain made the deer believe
all the songs would start again. Not to be—the fog
of silence iced the air with only memories.

    leaving
    the old life behind ::
    cymbals

Talent Show

After pulling on the Tripp pants and fight boots, the x-
straps and studded leather, she paints her face in
Mehron clown white, so that when she sits in the spot-
light behind a borrowed drum kit, she is the ghost of the
moon above the sharpness of stars, with every crash of
the cymbals leaving her old life behind.

    punk rock
    the tail-rattle
    of a gopher snake

To Go

I was never much of a gopher—too punk rock to walk straight; instead I snaked between the lines. Just like the time I was sent to fetch coffee for the office. Six lattes or was it seven? Non-fat? Was one of them tea with lemon? Behind me, that awkward tail of tapping toes; one man posed with his keys aloft to rattle right at me. Even despite the cardboard caddy, I spilled them all. Hot! Only then I noticed they'd misspelled and written *catty*.

steam train whispers in your ear

Tracks

Steam whispers from the electric kettle. The last of the snow melts from the cherry blossoms. In a branch, a Dark-eyed Junco calls and calls to your ear the whole of its three-note album, training you not to listen.

    the hours
    a line of boxcars
    empty or full

Roots

I marched out to the forest, followed
by a line of *Boxcar Children* books,
having packed a pail full of hours.
I ate an orange and then pulled
wild onions from the earth—
a mix of Georgia clay, sand and dirt.
How, even raw, the skinny ones
smelled like soup. All the while reading,
racing the empty sky. Foraging
for the bottom of the pile,
where I found Frost alive.

every word pages every word

The Flow

Every word is water carving a canyon into the bedrock of the blank page. Every sound is snowmelt tumbling down the steep slopes of the headwater streams, over limestone and lithoglyph, over granite and quartz and schist, over the falls and the walls of the gorges, gaining speed as they gather stones into chisels, rocks into drills, whirling into potholes and plunge pools, pulling up soil and sediment, uprooting trees, eroding the banks, overwhelming the estuaries with a churning foam of debris, each word indistinguishable in the froth of the loam, pages and pages pouring out from a singular mouth into the vast indifference of the sea.

brainstorm without an um
                                                brella

Rainbow

Even without a forecast, the best way to brainstorm
is with a cloud, so I scrawled an oval on a blank page,
leather bound. Determined, wrote "my life" in the center—
unabashed, in bold, black Sharpie. Every squiggly line
squeaked towards the next little storm. College, careers,
kids, and so many poems. How the clouds held a rope
as we crossed lanes of lightning. And, sometimes,
when the wind was just right, my umbrella
couldn't really help but turn into a kite.

                    c o n f e t t i
        free will   choose

After the Game

Anything can be a confetti. Sugar, rice, autumn leaves, bitter people. They flutter down like free-fall kites who've lost their wind, landing on the lawn in heaps of nylon and polyester, their tangled cords only half the mess. And who will choose to sweep and rake and drag them into piles for the trucks that come on Tuesday?

    laundry day
    another spin
    of the kaleidoscope

Pair

Early morning in the airplane's boarding line.
Outside, two birds on a wire, waiting for the first
glint of a worm's head or tail. I trace a jolt of sun
to a single woman's laugh, which spins the gray
in such a way that a bellows spurs a flame. And
that ignites more laughter—another kaleidoscope
of bells. After all, it isn't laundry day. Instead,
I wear ripped jeans that I wish to throw away.

    one sock
    worn inside out—
    seams
    I miss you

Cork

You sock the ball so hard the seams split clean from their red stitching, and that strand of string they wind around the inside starts leaking out in frayed strips of gray cotton. We'll keep playing, though, the rawhide worn into a soft purse that flies like a shot bird through the open field. I'll catch them all, every deep flyball. Neither one of us will miss until there's nothing left to miss.

high
sky
above
our
small
est
sha
dow

Split

While I was away, the birds forgot
about me in the Woodlands. Now
they flutter to the feeder, only to fly
back; all their feathers unfolding—
such angry fingers foisted to the sky.
First, a finch descends to the copper bar;
pauses just barely above. I did my best
impression. Became a hummingbird.
Now the others eye me from the trees;
chattering. A high flash of red, a gasp of
blue. Then the smallest shadow falls
on our feet, followed by the cracking
of so many sunflower seeds.

    woke
    up on the wrong side
    of the country

Hitchhikers

Get woke, then smoke, he said without saying, a city boy gone country music, one earbud left in his right ear. He'd looked cold on the shoulder. A penny for your oughts? I asked when he got in, but there were far too many. He was the kind of kid who couldn't hit the wrong side of a barn, forever unready to rake the ice. Ship up or shape out, someone clearly had told him. I think it was himself. I dropped him off on the short end of a long pier. The higher pass hadn't opened for the year.

riding shotgun
with our opinions

Compartmentalize

Maybe the way to do it is to seal
the leftovers of myself away; jump
inside glass tupperware, hugging a
shotgun. Then, when my opinions

start to bubble up—to ferment like the
whine no one asked for—I will shoot
out with our champagne. Imagine how
the glass would shatter; diamonds

digging new rings on the pine floor.
And imagine how spilled spaghetti
would no longer make me shout,
What the hell is this all for?

a tackle box | full of | impersonators

Hound Dogs

On the 89th anniversary of his birth, 89 Elvis impersonators tackled the slopes of the nearby ski resort. Someone had organized a photo-op, and the news crews loved it, all four networks broadcasting live from base-level at noon. Jump- suit-era Elvis was the obvious favorite—wool and gaberdine for the warmth, rhinestones for the glitter in the winter sun. So were the mogul runs, Elvis after Elvis gyrating down the mountain. That night, every restaurant in town was a box full of after-show Elvises, red-faced and wind-burned, real sweat greasing their ducktails and jelly-rolled hair. Too tired for fake accents, they laughed in their own voices, each one now unique, an uncanny chorus of howling drunks so completely off-key that everyone here still marvels at the harmony.

rabbit-hopping through the neighborhood gossip

Iron Man

Today there's a triathlon in the neighborhood. We cheer
for the wet runners as they crush cups of water, one
asking for ice to dump down his back. Imagine that.
Running and swimming and biking for one hundred
and forty miles—except here's a girl rabbit-hopping
the fence. Now she's jogging right beside them, turns
that into a sprint before she dives behind cones. Floats
behind a door. The next time we pass her, she's darting—
hot pink Spandex flapping out from a bush. Am I the
only one who looked? Do the others see her through
their windows? Do they gossip with the Gatorade
wondering if she even partook?

    deadlifting—
    I max out the bar
    with poems

Past Story

So many poems about the dead lifting the damp lid of the land with their dirty palms. So many movies on our 80-foot IMAX screens showing their slow shuffle into dust. We pretend the dead are more alive than we did when they were living. But they don't write the poems. They can't hear their own psalms. And probably what they'd want is to break the bars and drag us out of our tiny windows to tell us all the ways that we've gone wrong. That we should hold each other like we hold our phones. The way they do the rocks and the roots and the stones.

> silent film
> covering the earth
> from space

After the Credits

Sometimes I pause to see
this film between us—

squint to imagine these miles
as a perforated roll, unwinding

on a continuous scroll. We are
an ever-unfurling vine. We left

the negatives behind. We curl
across the country, covering

the earth with seeds. I was silent
when I first saw you; confused

a life with TV static. Blank
subtitles. But in your basket,

you brought me a picnic
of words. Where there once

was only space, now watch
these wildflowers stir.

laying the plot lines with you

Theories of Lift

You plot a poem, laying the little ramp of the first few lines so it faces head-on whatever wind can be seen in the weathervane. Then pedal, pumping over the ribcage of wooden planks with that ripchord rhythm as your wake. When you reach the air, it doesn't matter if the story is one of mass and momentum. It doesn't matter what Bernoulli said about fluid pressure, or the altered vibration of n-dimensional strings. In the end, it's just easy to fly. And they are such colorful things.

you and I
pinned together
the kite flips

About the Authors

Timothy Green is the editor of *Rattle* magazine, a fact which Katie Dozier is grateful for—particularly as he published her first poem in print! Before that, he grew up in Rochester, New York, and became known as the dude whose car doubled as a used sporting goods store. Katie bounced around the South in her early years, and kicked off a poker career while studying poetry at Florida State University. Years later, thanks to Tim's tireless promotion of unpretentious poetry with the weekly *Rattlecast* and *Critique of the Week*—and Katie's desire to be the best poet possible—they found each other! Now, Katie is a series editor for her favorite poetry magazine, and co-hosts the Prompt Lines on the *Rattlecast*. She also hosts and produces the *The Poetry Space_*, which Tim co-hosts. They enjoy speaking at NFT conferences as well as the less-blockchained world of traditional poetry, and going for long bike rides on the trails in The Woodlands, Texas—after which Timothy makes the best lasagna. Katie has a secret cookie recipe—but please don't tell anyone. This is their first book of the many they will write together.

www.ingramcontent.com/pod-product-compliance
Lightning Source LLC
LaVergne TN
LVHW051431080426
835508LV00022B/3342